Greater
things

I Cor 2:9

toby slough

normal

ISBN 978-0-9800321-2-3

Published by Cross Timbers Community Church, Argyle Texas
Printed by Mira Self Publishing, in the United States of America
For information or permissions, go to www.crosstimberschurch.org
www.normalthebook.com

All photography used by permission
Photography by Kimberly McCauley and Matt Doane
Design and layout by Ryan Colón and Andrea Schmid

Normal
by Toby Slough
© 2009

Dedicated to **Akbar**,

the little boy who captured my heart
and opened it wide to the
fatherless of the world.

GOODNIGHT RED LIGHT

All the proceeds from this book will go to rescue girls from Asia's largest red-light district. By purchasing this book, you will be partnering with Sower of Seeds International and others who are doing what is "normal" for followers of Christ.

Poverty has many expressions of abuse but none are perhaps as devastating to the human heart as "sex slavery". Little girls are bought, stolen or sold by people who prey upon them as a source of livelihood. Girls are often thrown in cages or locked in rooms for up to three years where they are repeatedly abused and tortured until they lose all will to run away. Then they are made to stand in the street, selling themselves for almost nothing...

Asia's largest red-light district:

Three square kilometers crammed with an estimated 40,000 women working its 24 lanes, earning at least $200 million a year in revenue for their traffickers, where 95% of the children of prostituted women become prostitutes, where children are trafficked into abuse and violence daily, where 73.7% of all girls trapped inside the brothel system must be rescued if they are ever to reach the outside world again... The world has forgotten them, but God hasn't.

$1,928 rescues and provides one year of care for a girl

$1,028 rescues and provides for 6 months of care

$ 578 rescues and supports a girl for 3 months

$ 150 supports a rescued girl for one month

$ 128 rescues one girl out of the red light district.

TO MAKE AN ADDITIONAL DONATION, GO TO www.sowerofseeds.org/rescue.

Thank you for being a part of rescuing these girls.

CONTENTS

So...

What is normal?

Who decides it?

Is it wearing jeans?

Driving an S.U.V.?

Two kids?

Three kids?

1.5 kids and two dogs?

Hamburgers?

Hot dogs?

Apple pie?

Do you even know any normal people?

I wonder what makes them normal.

Maybe because they

"behave" or they're nice, quiet, calm, simple.

You know...

they're normal.

They don't dance weird, sing weird, work weird, talk weird, act weird. Can we try to define normal for a second?

There were some crazy guys back in the day who did some not so "normal" stuff.

At least not according to our definition.

But what if that stuff...

you know, helping each other out, listening to God's voice (and actually obeying), healing the sick, feeding the

hungry, praying and actually seeing results...

What if that stuff is normal?

What if we're the weird ones?

CHAPTER ONE

SOMETHING IS DIFFERENT

CHANGE IS NORMAL

Have you ever seen the inkblots that psychologists use to test their patients? Officially, it's known as the Rorschach test. They ask the question, "What do you see?"

Sometimes I think we approach the Bible that way. Like it's one giant inkblot and we're left to decipher what it means, what it's supposed to be and marvel at its mystery. For example, we look at the Book of Acts and say stuff like, "Well that's interesting. I wonder why they did that?" or "I wonder what that's supposed to mean?" We look at life in the Kingdom and try to figure out what applies to us, what doesn't make sense, and scratch our heads about it. We treat it like it's something to overanalyze, but maybe what we read and "decipher" is more normal than we think.

Acts is kinda the "that was then, this is now" of the Bible. Let's be honest, it's not like we're all walking the streets healing the blind, telling the paraplegics to walk and getting arrested in Starbucks for praying over our berry bran muffin.

To read the book of Acts and really understand its content, you have to know some history. Let's start with this. The book of Acts was written by Luke. Luke is best known for writing one of the four gospels — the Gospel of Luke.

When the letters circled around through the little house churches that were growing up during that time, the book of Luke and the book of Acts were often paired and sent together. They were almost seen as one book, two volumes. In order to understand the book of Acts, you really need to read the book of Luke.

I'm contending that what you read in the book of Acts is normal, and what we live isn't. So it comes back to this — what is normal?

Let me shatter some myths about what many of you think when you hear the word "normal". Usually it's associated with "ordinary," "average," or "routine," but I'm not talking about average or ordinary. Normal is what you know as through your experiences.

Mika and I got married when we were both 21 years old. Going in, I had 21 years of how I thought life was supposed to be lived. You know — there's a way you roll up the toothpaste, a way you put things away, a time you eat, a way you do Christmas and how I do it is normal. Here's where the storm came in for Mika and I. She had 21 years of doing stuff, and her normal wasn't my normal so I decided she was weird, and she decided I was weird.

We had to take her 21 years of living and culture and my 21 years of my experiences and we needed to make a new normal.

Maybe it's time to make a new normal. Some of you have decided that the way your life operates is the way life is supposed to be. I think one of the reasons God gave us the book of Acts is because without it, we wouldn't know what life is supposed to look like after Jesus ascends into Heaven. The life that Jesus introduced, this new life is lived out in the book of Acts. Those things that seem supernatural, weird and "out there" to us are actually the norm. They are the expected pattern of how God calls us to live.

What does God say is normal?

Before I take you to Luke 22, let's look at what has happened. Jesus is preparing for His impending death. He has set His face toward Jerusalem. He's been in the upper room. He's told His disciples He's going to die.

He has spent His time in the Garden of Gethsemane, face down in the dirt, and begged God to take this cup from Him. All His friends have fallen asleep and He wakes them as the torches start coming into the garden. The guards arrest Jesus, Peter cuts off the guard's ear, Jesus puts the guard's ear back on, and the guard still takes Jesus into custody. (That I'll never understand. If somebody cuts my ear off and Jesus puts it back on, I'm not arresting the guy who heals me.) Jesus is led off before the governmental body to be sentenced to death. He has been hinting all along that it's going to get tough for the disciples.

One of the reasons I like Peter is because he's a lot like me and sometimes he says lots of things before he thinks. At the last supper, Jesus said in a matter of words "Hey guys. It's gonna get tough and some of you are going to deny me." He was talking about Judas who was going to betray Him but overenthusiastic Peter jumps out there and says, "Everybody else may deny you, but you can count on me!"

Now here we are in Luke 22. The Bible does a "scene within a scene." Jesus is under arrest, getting sentenced, the local crowds have gathered and the whole city is buzzing with what's happening. The scene turns to Peter. Here's the sentence that has gripped my soul for 20 years:

"And Peter followed him at a distance." Luke 22:54, NLT

Don't simply see what Peter is doing, but look into what Peter is thinking. Essentially it's

"Jesus, I'm not going to leave you,

but I'm not going to lay it all out on the line for you either."

Does this strike a nerve with you?

It's not that uncommon.

"Jesus - I need enough of you to get to heaven, but I'll take care of the rest. Give me just enough of an injection to save my soul, but don't mess with my checkbook, don't mess with my schedule, don't mess with my relationships, don't put me in harm's way, don't make me take a risk and don't make me look stupid."

"I'll follow you Jesus, just let me follow you at a distance."

Back to our scene. *"The guards lit a fire in the middle of the courtyard and sat around it and Peter joined them there. A servant girl noticed him in the firelight and began staring at him. Finally she said, 'This man was one of Jesus' followers!' But Peter denied it. 'Woman,' he said. 'I don't even know him!'"* Luke 22:54-57, NLT

If you go on and read the rest of that chapter, Peter is called out two more times. People recognize him and point out that he was a follower of Christ, but both times he flat out denies it.

The last time someone asks him, the rooster crows. At this denial, Jesus happens to be close enough to hear it. The Bible tells us that with one glance from Jesus, Peter remembers the words from Him just earlier that day while they were having their last meal together. Just after Peter's exuberant promise to never deny Him, Christ said "Before the rooster crows today, you will disown me three times."

The Bible said when Peter recalled these words and realized his own failures, he wept bitterly.

As we all know, Jesus was sentenced, crucified and resurrected on the third day. On that day, He appeared to the disciples. Finally, in Luke 24, Jesus is taken up into Heaven. At that point, the angel declares to all the disciples who are still staring up into the clouds, "Go and make disciples of all nations." Go do what Jesus told you to do. It's now when the church begins to explode. The Holy Spirit falls on the day of Pentecost and a man emerges from the church, a voice for the followers of Christ.

It's Peter.

In Acts 4, Peter and John are out doing what they're supposed to do; talking about Jesus and spreading the Good News. In the wake of Christ's death and because of what the disciples were teaching, the government was not happy. They arrested Peter and John and brought them before the government council — the priests, the Sadducees, the leaders of the guard who had arrested Jesus — and decided to throw Peter and John in jail overnight.

I think it's interesting to note that Peter's worst fears are now being realized. This is exactly why he followed at a distance and why he denied his association with Christ to the peasant girl by the fire. He didn't want to go to jail. He didn't want to get caught up in the mess. Now it's happening. Here's the catch. They'll let him off the hook, if he'll just do what he did around the fire.

Here's what happens next: *Then Peter, filled with the Holy Spirit, said to them, "Rulers and elders of our people, are we being questioned today because we've done a good deed for a crippled man? Do you want to know how he was healed? Let me clearly state to all of you and to all the people of Israel that he was healed by the powerful name of Jesus Christ the Nazarene, the man you crucified but whom God raised from the dead. For Jesus is the one referred to in the Scriptures, where it says, 'The stone that you builders rejected has now become the cornerstone.' There is salvation in no one else! God has given no other name under heaven by which we must be saved." The members of the council were amazed when they saw the boldness of Peter and John, for they could see that they were ordinary men with no special training in the Scriptures. They also recognized them as men who had been with Jesus." Acts 4:8-13, NLT*

Now you tell me - is this the same guy? People must be thinking as these letters circulated through the churches, and they've just read about his denial and intimidation by the teenage Jewish peasant girl, and now they're reading about this guy. They knew the culture. They knew what was at stake. Now here he is boldly proclaiming the message of Christ. Don't just look at what he did. Look at his heart, look where his mind is and look at his character. You have to ask, who is this guy? This isn't an improved Peter. This is a brand new Peter.

Here are some things the Bible doesn't tell us that I wonder about.

I wonder, after that first night of denial, how Peter felt every time he heard a rooster crow. Have you ever pulled out an old record or CD, or catch a song on the radio that you used to listen to? You know, the song that was "your song" in high school or college, or from places where you were doing things you maybe shouldn't have been doing...It brings up the memory, right?

I just wonder the level of guilt and shame and condemnation that Peter felt every time that bird crowed. Even before Jesus met him on the beach (John 21), I wonder how many church people reminded Peter of his failure. When he was out encouraging, challenging, talking about Christ, I can almost picture people saying, "Who are you to tell us this?"

I wonder how many nights, Peter lay in his bed wondering if his denial of Christ would be the headline of his life. If Peter ever felt like his life and ministry, as he knew it, was over because he had done "that". Did Peter in the midst of those moments ever feel like giving up? That he had done the worst possible thing, was doomed and could never change?

From Genesis to Revelation, the theme of scripture is that God is in the "making new" business. In Christ we are made new and the book of Acts shows you that your life changing and the process of being transformed from the inside out, seeing things differently, responding differently, believing differently... and not an improved heart but a new heart... that is normal.

Knowing Christ and being the same 10 years later is not normal. However, that's not what our world says and for many of us, that has not been our experience. The truth in the word of God is that transformation in the Kingdom is normal.

Peter, a distant follower, who went back on his word and denied Christ at the drop of a hat transformed to a confident, bold disciple of Christ who didn't even cower under the threats of the government authorities and religious leaders. Ultimately, we shouldn't be surprised that the work of Christ changed him into a completely different man. Because that is normal. It's standard. It is the pattern. For every believer.

Is that normal for you?

CHAPTER TWO

CHANGING THE WAY WE THINK ABOUT CHANGE

Start at Ephesians 2:10 (NLT): *"For we are God's masterpiece. He has created us anew in Christ Jesus, so we can do the good things he planned for us long ago."*

We are God's masterpiece. Some versions say "workmanship." I am God's project. I'm not a self-improvement project. I am a God-improvement project. Whether or not I notice it in my day to day life, from the beginning of time, God had a destiny for me. That destiny is holiness and perfection and effectiveness in his Kingdom.

BE BETTER

ONE STEP TO HAPPINESS

4 1/2 WAYS TO PAINT A SMILE

8 STEPS FOR A HAPPY LIFE

two more steps & you're there

5 STEPS TOWARD A BETTER YOU

EAT LESS & FEEL BLESSED

FEEL BEAUTIFUL IN ZERO TO 60 SECONDS

YOU'RE STRONG, YOU'RE POWERFUL

HOW TO FIX YOURSELF ...IN 3 STEPS

I was a white kid who didn't move very fast playing defensive back in the town of Angelton, Texas. We played against schools like Galveston Ball and LaMarque High School; really athletic, really fast teams. I was struggling and I had about six coaches who were letting me know it. They weren't kindly letting me know. They were doing what coaches did back in the '80s. They were finding any way they could to humiliate me, screaming "Slough you're a girl!"... just whatever they could come up with.

It was Coach Morgan who really changed my life. It was before my sophomore year and I was trying out for the varsity team. I was not doing well but really wanted to. Coach Morgan took me aside one day in practice and said, "Toby, I know those guys are yelling at you but I believe in you. I believe you're a good football player. I believe you can do this."

He took me by the shoulders, looked me in the eyes and said, "I don't want you to listen to those guys. I want you to hear me.

Here's who you are. Here's what you can do."

I went home that night, a 16-year-old insecure sophomore kid whose whole world was about football, and I laid in my bed with those words ringing through my head and my heart. He was calling the football player out in me. The next time I went back out on the field, I started playing better. Why? Because he wasn't correcting my behavior, he was speaking instead to my identity.

This is the next part of transformation and we hear it straight from Jesus.

"I am the true grapevine, and my Father is the gardener. He cuts off every branch of mine that doesn't produce fruit, and he prunes the branches that do bear fruit so they will produce even more. You have already been pruned and purified by the message I have given you. Remain in me, and I will remain in you. For a branch cannot produce fruit if it is severed from the vine, and you cannot be fruitful unless you remain in me. Yes, I am the vine; you are the branches. Those who remain in me, and I in them, will produce much fruit. For apart from me you can do nothing." John 15:1-5, NLT

So you want the secret to a transformed life? Ready? Abiding in Christ.

Doesn't it seem like there needs to be something else we need to do?

It's that simple — Jesus says, connect to me, abide in me, find your source in me, and I will fruitfully change your life. So maybe the answer isn't the seven steps to a fruitful transformed Christian life…

Maybe it's finding new creative ways to, as Richard Foster calls, "living out of your center."

Find new creative ways
to stay connected to Jesus Christ.

How do I change what I believe?

Why is that so important? Just like Coach Morgan, Jesus will always go beyond the behavior and speak straight into our identity. When we talk about change, we always begin at a behavioral level. When I say "you need to change", what do you immediately think of? Probably your behavior. Quit this. Start this. Don't do this. Do this.

Change at a behavioral level works for awhile. New Year's resolutions are a perfect example. You resolve to change your behavior and by March you've already tried five different diets. Why is change at a behavioral level so temporal? Because our behavior is fueled out of what we believe. A behavioral change works for awhile but it's not sustainable if what you believe doesn't change.

So how do I change what I believe? Good question. Jesus doesn't want to talk to you at a behavioral level. However, He doesn't even want to talk to you at a belief level. He wants to talk to you about your identity. When your identity changes, your beliefs change and the result is that your behavior changes. Coach Morgan knew if he could change the way I saw myself, then I would believe that I was a better player,

which in turn, would make me a better player. This is what I missed for so long in my walk with Christ. I felt like I was hitting a wall, but it was at a behavioral level. Through crisis 15 years ago, God began to change my beliefs. The real change came when Jesus, not a preacher, not a friend, but Jesus began to show me WHO I am in Christ.

When Jesus says abide in me and remain in me, He is saying "Stick close. Only I can speak into your heart." When we remain close to Him and truth infiltrates our souls, our identities begin to change. Then, what we believe begins to change, and all the do's and don'ts... they take care of themselves. It's this — because of who I am, here's how I believe and here's how I'll respond. When that happens, we are transformed...that's normal.

It was true for Peter and it's true for you. You're searching from book to book, conference to conference, church to church while what you're looking for will only be found by abiding in Christ. He's still connecting with screw-ups like me and He's still calling it out of people's lives. He doesn't want to improve you. He wants to change you.

CHAPTER THREE

WHEN THE SKY IS FALLING

COURAGE IN UNCERTAIN TIMES IS NORMAL

"And now, O Lord, hear their threats, and give us, your servants, great boldness in preaching your word. Stretch out your hand with healing power; may miraculous signs and wonders be done through the name of your holy servant Jesus." — Acts 4:29-30

Back to Peter in Acts. We've just read about how Peter and John were arrested by the authorities and they've been thrown in jail.

Put yourself in the shoes of one of the early followers of Christ. Your leaders have been thrown in jail. You and everyone else who is part of the movement are praying for their release. At this point, you're not even guaranteed that the authorities aren't going to bang down your front door.

Here's the thing. If you just quit talking about Jesus, then everything will be fine. If not, they're coming after you.

Imagine this group of people. They were faced with a choice. Deny Christ and they'd be fine. Don't and they were facing the very real chance that their whole family would be ripped apart. The authorities could've taxed their tunics off and taken all of their physical property. The government posed a threat to radically destroy their lives. This is not just a small local leader. They were faced with the oppression of the entire Roman Government.

Step in their shoes. Imagine when it comes time to pray, what do you think is going to come out of your mouth? Me? I would've prayed David's prayer... something along the lines of "Knock out the teeth of my enemies. God — take care of these guys! We're right they're wrong. Do something to them!"

Instead, here's what those early followers of Christ prayed —"*And now, O Lord, hear their threats, and give us, your servants, great boldness in preaching your word. Stretch out your hand with healing power; may miraculous signs and wonders be done through the name of your holy servant Jesus.*" Acts 4:29-30

Don't do something to them, do something to me. Their prayer is "don't fix everything around me. Do something in me."

"After this prayer, the meeting place shook, and they were all filled with the Holy Spirit. Then they preached the word of God with boldness." Acts 4:31

Have you ever
faced uncertainty?

Ever found yourself in a financial storm? Has your marriage ever hit rock bottom? Maybe your kids are out of control ... they could go either way, or they have gone a way you didn't want them to go. The one thing we are certain about is that we don't like uncertain things in our lives. We like things laid out in a plan. It's human nature. We like to know the map; that if A happens then B happens then C is going to happen. One of the travesties of the church, in my opinion, is that we have taught people to believe that if you come to Christ, take these five planned steps, then God is always going to do "this". We've somehow tried to program Christianity. One of my favorite old sayings that I like to make fun of is:

"The safest place to be is in the will of God."

That's bull! What the Bible teaches is that one of the most dangerous places to be is right in the will of God. It is a safe place spiritually speaking, but there's nothing certain in the Christian life other than the things I'm about to talk about...

One of my friends tells a story about when he was 16 and he had finally scraped together enough money to buy a truck. He describes this black truck as the one he loved. He took precious care of it, and sunk every last penny he had into making it the truck of his dreams. Then one sad day, on his way to school, smoke started to spill out of the engine block. Panicked, he pulled over to the side of the road and realized his truck was on fire. The way he says it,

"My God died that day, on the side of the road in Fort Worth, Texas, right outside of my High School."

If your god is your house, and your house value has dropped in half, you're not going to have courage because your god is dying. If your god is your kid's achievement or their ability to do well on the sports field, in the classroom, or in the band, and they don't do so well, your confidence is going to wane because your god is dying. If your god is your 401K, your retirement plan or what's happening on Wall Street, and it all starts to sink, it means that your god is in New York City and not reigning in heaven.

This is our problem. The transformation you see of the men and women in Acts 4 happens because their focus was off of their circumstances and their focus was on God. They believed that He was more than enough.

Their lives were not based in what was happening around them. They believed that Jesus was going to make a real difference in their lives. I'm not saying "don't worry." If you're like me, you might worry about worrying too much. Instead, give your worry to Christ. I'm not saying be a spiritual weirdo but when it comes, give it to Jesus. Sometimes trusting and having courage is moment by moment and an hour by hour thing.

When life discourages you, do you ever feel alone? When you're facing something, does it ever feel like you're the only one facing it and no one would ever understand it? It would have been easy for those people in Acts 4 to feel this way. Instead, their courage came from the understanding that they weren't alone because the Holy Spirit had taken up residence in their hearts.

The greatest courage of the human heart is to take one more step when you don't feel like you have another step in you because the Holy Spirit is in you.

God will provide for you but sometimes it's one step and one day at a time. It is only revealed by the Holy Spirit. They had a risen reigning Christ above them, Holy Spirit in them and they had a community of faith around them. They were encouraging one another.

I don't believe that this was like a fairytale land. I don't believe that everyone was fired up like "OK! Let's go get thrown in jail! Let's get beat up!" Some were filled with fear. Some were filled with faith.

The Bible teaches me that when I don't have faith, your gift of faith can affect my life. There can be moments when you won't have it and I will. Take a look around you. Have you surrounded yourself with people who only give you bad news? Are they the running ticker from the news channel? What you need is people around you who will say "The good news is, the bad news is wrong! Remember what Jesus promised. Remember who you are in Christ. God promises to meet your needs."

encourage **to inspire with courage, spirit, or hope**

Maybe your issue is not the stock market. Maybe the issue is your god is too small, your spirit is too weak and you don't have people around you speaking truth into your life because you've isolated yourself. The end result of their courage is that they did something. How did they fight their fear? They did something. If you're facing an uncertain future, step out and do something for somebody else. The enemy wants to isolate you and get your focus on you and your situation. It's a Bermuda Triangle. Live normally. Believe there's a Jesus above you, a Spirit within you, build a community around you and make a difference in somebody's life. That's normal.

Jesus above them.
Holy Spirit in them.
Community around them.

CHAPTER FOUR

LISTEN CLOSELY

HEARING FROM GOD IS NORMAL

"It is actually best for you that I go away, because if I don't, the Counselor won't come. If I do go away, he will come because I will send him to you.... When the Spirit of truth comes, he will guide you into all truth. He will not be presenting his own ideas; he will be telling you what he has heard. He will tell you about the future."—John 16:7, 13. NLT

In Acts 1, Jesus ascends into Heaven. The story tells us that some of the disciples continued to "strain their eyes" to try and see Him in the clouds. Two angels showed up and basically said "Quit staring at the sky and go do what Jesus said to do."

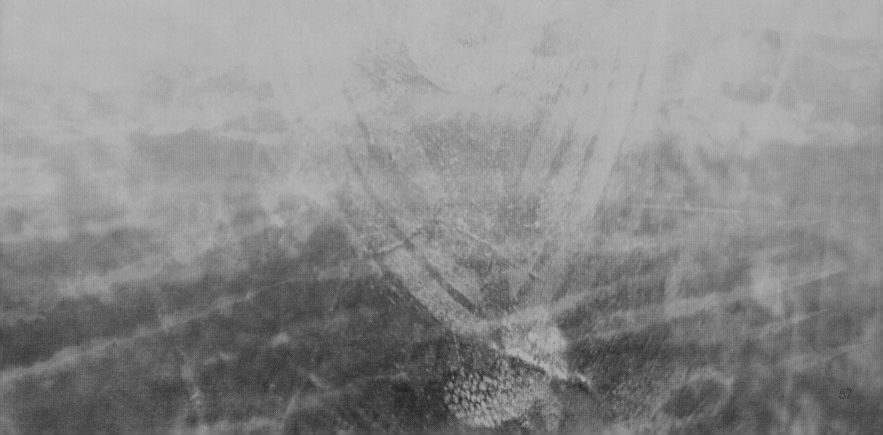

As it turns out, they are facing a very practical problem. They are one disciple short because one disciple sold Jesus out. (His name? Judas. It's why we don't name our kids "Judas". He wasn't such a great guy.) So before they can continue on to do what Christ said, the disciples have to choose a new member for their group.

"So now we must choose another man to take Judas's place. It must be someone who has been with us all the time that we were with the Lord Jesus." Acts 1:21

Their natural response? God, speak to us and tell us what we're supposed to do.

You promised us you were going to be here for us.

This is the pattern we see all over Acts. Every chapter, except for Acts 17, shows God speaking supernaturally into the lives of His disciples. In Acts 2, the Holy Spirit comes. These guys are clearly affected and everyone in town just assumes, "Well these guys must be drunk." Peter says, "They're not drunk.. it's 9 in the morning." Mind you, this is long before "it's 5 o'clock somewhere."

Then Peter, this unschooled, ordinary, not very smart guy, begins to show them how this was a fulfillment of a prophecy. Look at it this way — this biker dude who is really a rough and tough guy begins to elementally put together Old and New Testament prophecy.

Here's my question... Where did he get that from? Did he just get smart all of a sudden? No... God gave that to him.

"There was also a man named Ananias who, with his wife, Sapphira, sold some property. He brought part of the money to the apostles, but he claimed it was the full amount. His wife had agreed to this deception. Then Peter said, 'Ananias, why has Satan filled your heart? You lied to the Holy Spirit, and you kept some of the money for yourself. The property was yours to sell or not sell, as you wished. And after selling it, the money was yours to give away. How could you do a thing like this? You weren't lying to us but to God.' As soon as Ananias heard these words, he fell to the floor and died. Everyone who heard about it was terrified. Then some young men wrapped him in a sheet and took him out and buried him. About three hours later his wife came in, not knowing what had happened. Peter asked her, 'Was this the price you and your husband received for your land?' 'Yes,' she replied, 'that was the price.' And Peter said, 'How could the two of you even think of doing a thing like this – conspiring together to test the Spirit of the Lord? Just outside that door are the young men who buried your husband, and they will carry you out, too.' Instantly, she fell to the floor and died. When the young men came in and saw that she was dead, they carried her out and buried her beside her husband." Acts 5:1-10

The question is, how did Peter know? God spoke to him. It was John 14, 15 & 16... just living it out.

In Acts 10:9, Peter is staying at a house in Joppa. He is out on the roof around noon to pray. For starters, you need to understand in that culture the Jews are religiously racist. They believe they're the chosen ones. They're all in on the gospel, but the gospel is just for them. That's what the Bible says. Peter is sold out on this belief.

So back to the roof. He's out there and the Bible says he falls into a "trance", a dream-like state. He sees the sky open and all the food that any self-respecting Jew is not supposed to eat comes down on a sheet. It's like a whacked out dream. He hears a voice (who is God) that says, "Hey you need to kill and eat these things." Peter replies, "I'm a good Jew! I don't eat that stuff." God answers to him, "It's time for you to eat it." Peter was about to see and witness that the gospel is not just for the Jews, but it's also for the Gentiles. He went from there and carried this message to the people and followers of Christ. Over and over again, God speaks, the people hear and they act on it.

That's normal.

True confession — do you get nervous or weirded out when someone starts talking about "hearing from God"? It makes a lot of people nervous. Why? Because we've been abused by it through the years. I know plenty of people who have had the "God told me to tell you thing" thrown in their face so they could be manipulated to do what someone else wanted them to do. In Christian circles, "God told me" is the ultimate trump card.

We've seen it abused and then our response is to just back away from it. Maybe we get nervous because we have a sense that other people have heard from God and we haven't. Deep down inside we feel inferior and we don't like that very much. So instead of trying to hear from God, we decide, "I have a brain, I have a Bible, I'll just figure it out."

I don't like looking silly or foolish. Here's an idea — you don't have to be a weirdo. I think you can follow God, and you can have all the gifts of the Spirit and you don't have to be "that guy". Hearing from God doesn't have to be weird.

Here are the biggest questions you'll have to face:

Am I going to risk abuse?

Am I going to risk missing God?

Am I going to risk wanting something so badly that I make God in my own image?

Am I going to risk all of those things and still try to hear God and being led by God?

Or am I going to do it on my own?

Am I going to try and figure it out for myself?

Am I going to say "God I don't need to hear from you?

I've decided it's normal to hear God and be led by His spirit in practical ways. Sometimes it is different. Sometimes His ways aren't my ways and it doesn't always go the way I think it's going to go.

practical ways.
it doesn't always

God in my own image?
to hear God and being led by God?

CHAPTER FIVE

COMMON MISCONCEPTIONS

IN OTHER WORDS, WHY YOU MIGHT THINK YOU CAN'T HEAR FROM GOD

MYTH NUMBER 1
Hearing God means hearing an audible voice.

Lots of people think this way. It's the idea that "If I haven't heard an audible voice, then I haven't heard God." Hearing an audible voice is the exception, not the rule. All over the Bible, God speaks through dreams, visions and prophets. God uses all creative means out there to speak to people. Personally, I have never heard the audible voice of God.

I'm not an artist and I don't think in pictures, so very rarely does God speak to me through art or dreams. For me, it's a thought. I'll say something like, "Lord speak to me today. I'm asking about this, etc..." then a thought will come into my mind and I'm trusting that that's God speaking to me.

Now the enemy speaks too, so that's why I need to stay in the Word and know that God will never lead me to do something outside of His Word. Hearing God can happen through a thought. It's an impression. I'm so relational in nature that God will even use situations to speak to me. He'll put me in an interaction and I'll realize something is happening that is more than just what's happening. I notice that God puts me in those moments to speak truth to me.

We seriously need to get off this thing that God is an audible voice and begin to be available and open to all these frequencies on which God is speaking.

I heard this illustration once from my friend, Bob Hamp... In whatever you room you are sitting in right now, every radio station in your area is in that room too. All you need is a tuner. With the right tuner, at the right frequency, you can hear them all. In the same way, God is speaking through all different frequencies. We're hung up thinking it has to be a certain way and sound like something specific. When we don't hear it, we just turn the tuner off.

God can use music, art, creation, a friend...

MYTH NUMBER 2
You just "know" how to do it.

Hearing God is a learned trait. You have to practice and learn how to hear God. Is your prayer life any deeper or richer than it was five years ago? (If not, see chapter 2). How did it happen? You prayed! I know the Bible much better than when I was 30 years old. How did that happen? I read it.

How do you become a servant? Serve people.

How do you hear God? Start listening.

Be wise, ask and hear, then take a step.

Hear, then take another step.

You gain confidence, you miss it, then step back.

MYTH NUMBER 3
Hearing God means I need to tell Him lots of stuff first.

Ok, so maybe that's not what we're actually thinking, but that's what our actions are saying. My prayer life used to be like checking out a grocery store.

Some of this.

A little of this.

Some of this...

In Jesus name, Amen.

And then I wondered why I didn't hear God speak! Is your prayer life lots of talking and no listening?

Prayer is a conversation and a conversation goes both ways. So start by asking God questions. Most of the time we start at the wrong place. We start by asking God directional questions. God begins to speak to us not at a directional level, but at an identity level. God wants you to get right who you are and who He is in your life. Once you begin to hear God tell you who you are and who He is, a lot of the directional questions take care of themselves.

There is one summer afternoon memory I will never forget. My son Ross was 18 at the time, getting ready to leave for his first year of college. At the time I was on my sabbatical, and was learning about all these new, revolutionary concepts about hearing from God, and God changing me at an identity level, not a behavioral level. I sat on the porch with him and shared all of these new to me concepts with him. I got to the part about asking God a question and listening to the answer. I said, "Why don't we try it?" He agreed to give it a try. So we bowed our heads and I said, "Lord, would you tell Ross something he needs to know about himself that he doesn't know, that might be keeping him from experiencing everything You have for him?" It was a really cool moment. I had my arm around him, and we both had our eyes closed. About two minutes into it, because I'm his daddy and a pastor, I started fish eyeing him. He wasn't saying anything, and I watched as just one tear hit the ground. It killed me to just wait and not ask him, but after another minute or so, he opened his eyes. I asked him what he heard and he said, "Dad, I just felt like I heard God say He thinks I'm a really good guy."

...revolutionary concepts about hearing from God, and God changing me at an identity level, not a behavioral level.

We both didn't know what he was about to face and experience at school. His whole world was about to change. New life. New friends. That word from God was what he needed.

Do you realize how passionate God is for intimacy with you? There is no possible way for you to want God as much as God wants you. God stood outside time and space and went to a cross and died so that He could be intimate with you. We sometimes live our lives as though God doesn't want to be part of it.

"God help me!"
He says, "I will. Just ask me."

You can hear God, every day
of your life. That is normal.

CHAPTER SIX

BRINGING WATER TO THE SLUMS

MEETING THE NEEDS OF OTHERS IS NORMAL

The first time I traveled to India, I learned a Kingdom Principle firsthand. I was there to see a the drilling of a well in an Indian slum that my church had helped to support. We were partnering with the work of Sower of Seeds International, and they had contracted with a well digging company. S.O.S. did all the logistics. The well digging crew had all their gear setup and ready.

At that point it was late in the evening and everyone backed up to let the little pastor of that slum move to the front. The whole slum had gathered to see what was happening. Nearly 15,000 people, a mixture of Muslims and Hindus, were craning their necks to see what this little man was going to say. He stood tall and shouted, "In the name of Jesus Christ of Nazareth, we bring you water to this slum today!"

"In the name of Jesus Christ of Nazareth,
we bring you water to this slum today."

79

For this group of people, who believed in all sorts of different gods and worshipped at little idol booths all over the slum, the news that a God was meeting a very physical need was a very big deal. Now people in this community are coming to Christ in record numbers because they're seeing that Jehovah God is the only God who is doing anything about their situation.

"All the believers devoted themselves to the apostles' teaching, and to fellowship, and to sharing in meals (including the Lord's Supper), and to prayer. A deep sense of awe came over them all, and the apostles performed many miraculous signs and wonders. And all the believers met together in one place and shared everything they had. They sold their property and possessions and shared the money with those in need. They worshiped together at the Temple each day, met in homes for the Lord's Supper, and shared their meals with great joy and generosity all the while praising God and enjoying the goodwill of all the people. And each day the Lord added to their fellowship those who were being saved." Acts 2:42-47

"All the believers were united in heart and mind. And they felt that what they owned was not their own, so they shared everything they had. The apostles testified powerfully to the resurrection of the Lord Jesus, and God's great blessing was upon them all. There were no needy people among them, because those who owned land or houses would sell them and bring the money to the apostles to give to those in need." Acts 4:32-35

Acts 2 lays things out pretty simply. The early church gathered together. They followed the teachings of Jesus Christ and devoted themselves to prayer and growing in their faith. They took care of one another. They took care of all the needs of the church and the end result of that was thousands came to know Jesus. What I love even more is that Luke, the writer of Acts, lets us know that this was not a one-time event. It was the heartbeat of the church. It was normal.

Here is an example of a community where people were regularly gathering, bringing what they had and leveraging their gifts into the lives of other people. I believe that this should be normal for us as believers... to bring what we have together and leverage everything into the lives of people.

Where did these early Christians learn this? If you look back in Luke 9, a familiar story, we watch as the disciples who are the church leaders in Acts experience an incredible miracle.

"The crowds found out where He was going, and they followed Him. He welcomed them and taught them about the Kingdom of God, and He healed those who were sick. Late in the afternoon the twelve disciples came to Him and said, 'Send the crowds away to the nearby villages and farms, so they can find food and lodging for the night. There is nothing to eat here in this remote place.' But Jesus said, 'You feed them.' 'But we have only five loaves of bread and two fish,' they answered. 'Or are you expecting us to go and buy enough food for this whole crowd?' For there were about 5,000 men there. Jesus replied, 'Tell them to sit down in groups of about fifty each.' So the people all sat down. Jesus took the five loaves and two fish, looked up toward heaven, and blessed them. Then, breaking the loaves into pieces, He kept giving the *bread and fish to the disciples so they could distribute it to the people. They all ate as much as they wanted, and afterward, the disciples picked up twelve baskets of leftovers!" Luke 9:11-17*

The disciples reacted in the way most people would have reacted. If there's a problem, just send people away to take care of their own problems. You know that American saying, "God helps those who help themselves." It's the American way. Pull yourself up by your own bootstraps. Grab your dream and if you work hard enough you can take care of yourself. It's the same thing the disciples were saying. In this case, the problem was the hunger. The disciples asked, "You want us to tell them to go get their own food?"

Jesus says, "No, I want you to feed them."

I love the strategic nature of Jesus' ministry. Jesus immediately makes a plan to break the group down into manageable numbers — groups of 50. Most of us miss the Kingdom principle Jesus is trying to teach here. Notice what He does: He breaks the loaves and fish and He gives the pieces to the disciples to hand out. We have to realize that the disciples haven't had anything to eat yet either. I can imagine that they're thinking, "Why would I waste this food on all these people? Maybe I can sneak some so that I get something to eat." Wouldn't that be something we'd do? We see all this need around us and our natural human tendency is to say "I'll just take care of myself. Need to make sure I get my slice of the pie." Instead, the disciples followed Jesus' principle and continued to break the pieces and give it out to the people. This process happened again and again. Take the food, break it in half, give it out. Break it in half again, give it out. Here is what's normal... understand that when God asks for what you have, if you will give it to somebody else, God will multiply it and leverage it in the lives of other people and even in your life.

This is something we are missing in America. We're scared. All of the market commentators and the political pundits have the freedom to forewarn and tell us that the sky is falling. Everyone is scrambling to hang on to their piece of bread. When Jesus moves in, He says "Want to live a normal life? Break it and give it to somebody else." I know that He will meet our needs and do "exceedingly above beyond what you could ever ask or imagine." There will be leftovers in the basket if you will have faith to break what you have and hand it to somebody else.

This is normal for a believer. The disciples lived this. They watched Jesus do it. So why wouldn't they, in the book of Acts, bring everything they have, and leverage it out for the needs of their community. It's amazing to me that NOBODY has need.

If I could package up what is happening in the slums in India where believers are meeting real needs, and bring that principle to action here in the States, I think the culture of American Christianity would change. We need to start pouring everything back into the lives of people who don't know Christ so they can see the Jesus who meets their needs.

my question for you is what do you need to break in half, share with somebody else?

That's normal and the reason we don't do it is because we're scared. We're scared that we're going to be left hanging.

"I tell you the truth, anyone who believes in me will do the same works I have done, and even greater works, because I am going to be with the Father." John 14:12

What did Jesus mean by "you are going to do greater things"? I don't think He meant that He was the JV and we are the Varsity.

The spirit of God lives in Christ and so everywhere He went, when an opportunity came up, He blessed somebody. He could touch someone and see healing. He could change someone's eternity every single day. How was Jesus limited? By time and space. That was one of the greatest sacrifices He made. How? He was limited to the people who could come in contact with Him. He was one man with two hands and two feet and did as much as He could on His own.

In John 14, He was saying that the spirit of God no longer resides solely in Christ.

It now can be in us. In me. In you.

Now it's not limited to one person. It's millions of people all around the world. There are some things that only God can do, but when we pray, sometimes it's us who are supposed to go, to give, to sacrifice, to send a check, to meet a need, to encourage someone, to speak truth, to provide a meal.

Not long ago at Cross Timbers, we were able to pay the utility bills for families in our church who had lost their jobs during the bad economy. Our overall "payout" that weekend was $24,600.

Personally, I didn't have $24,600 to give away, but my piece was part of it and together we did something that for some reason other people and even the media thought was radical. It's just Kingdom living. It's Jesus. It's the Bible. It's normal.

So to wrap this up —
Maybe your perspective
needs to change.
What you're looking at as "strange"
isn't so bizarre or unlikely after all.
To change and be transformed,
To have courage in uncertain times,
To hear from God,
To meet the needs of people...
This is normal.

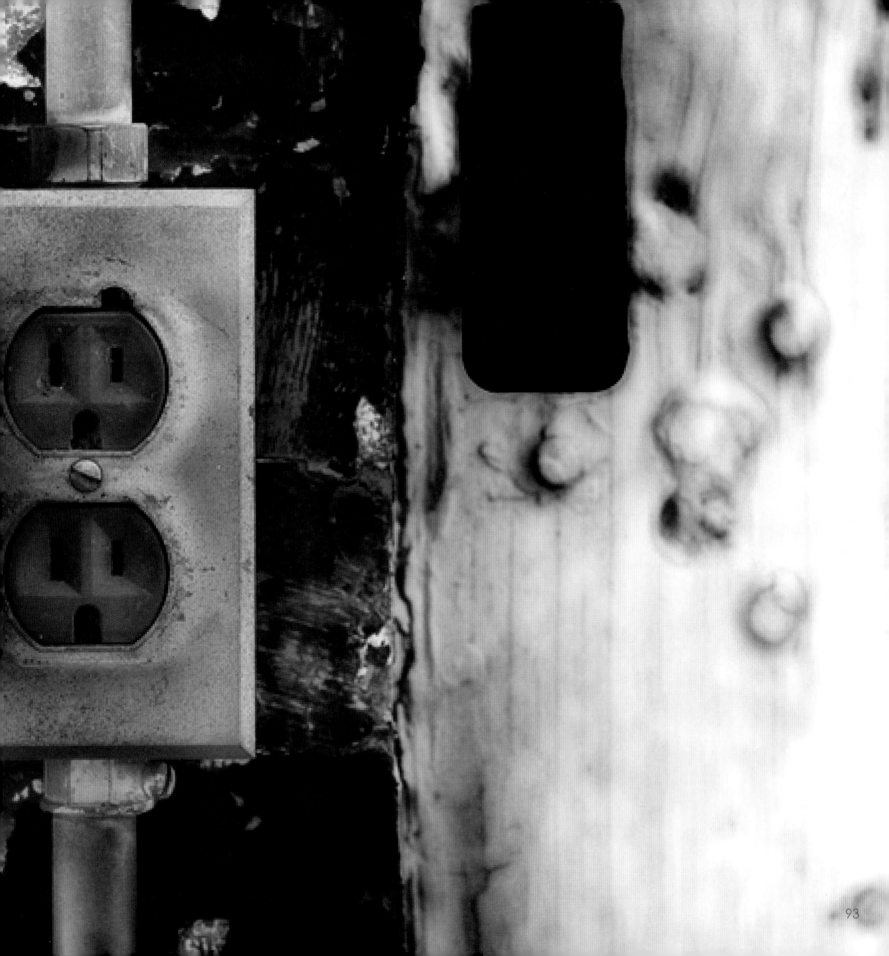

Maybe we're the weird ones.

Huh.